ERic
SAYS PLEASE

WRITTEN BY
iLLUSTRATED BY

This book is dedicated to my wonderful niece, Megan Hope.
My prayer is that Jesus would capture your heart and make
your life one big adventure!

thegoodbook
For children

Eric Says Please
© Dai Hankey / The Good Book Company 2017

'The Good Book For Children' is an imprint of The Good Book Company Ltd
Tel: 0333 123 0880   International: +44 (0) 208 942 0880   Email: info@thegoodbook.co.uk

UK: www.thegoodbook.co.uk North America: www.thegoodbook.com
Australia: www.thegoodbook.com.au New Zealand: www.thegoodbook.co.nz

Illustrated by Xavier Bonet / Design & Art Direction by André Parker

ISBN: 9781910307540   Printed in India

The door bell rang and up sprang mum.
"Eric!" she called. "Get a move on, son."

"Grandpa's here to take you to school."
"I'm ready!" chimed Eric. "And I look super cool!"

Grandpa smiled, "You certainly do.
Now, shall I tie your laces for you?"
"No thanks, Gramps, I don't need help.
I'm a big kid now - I can do it myself!"

But despite his twiddling, twirling and wrapping, Eric set off with his laces flapping!

He arrived at school and dashed to his class.
Mr Keane announced, "This morning's craft
Is a project making matchstick rafts!
If you need a hand, then please just ask."

"Thank you, Sir, but I don't need help.
I'm a genius, me - I can do it myself!"
And with those words Eric proceeded
To build the good ship "No Help Needed".

But when Mr Keane came over to check,
He found less of a raft and more of a wreck!
Eric's heart sank as soon as he'd shown it,
'Cos deep, deep down he knew that he'd blown it.

Sullen, subdued, in a sulky mood,
Eric waited in line for his food.
He stacked his tray but could barely move.
Miss Smith offered aid, but Eric refused.

"Thank you, Miss, but I don't need help.
I'm super-strong - I can do it myself!"

Then one step...
Two step...
Three step...
SLIP!!
Eric tripped...

His tray flipped... and whipped... and dipped...
Then SPLAT!!
It hit!

Miss Smith cleaned him up and refilled his tray.
"Eric, next time let me help, okay?"
"Thanks," said Eric, as he chewed on his chow,
"But I'll be just fine. I'm sorted now."

Later that day Eric popped out to play,
Determined to prove he was A-oKay.
He found a tree and started to climb,
Trembling, ascending an inch at a time...

Till knocky-kneed and shaky-handed,
"Yikes!" he gasped. "I think I'm stranded!"

On the ground his friend Billy Brown
Tried to work out how to get Eric down.
"Eric, hold on! I know what to do.
I'm gonna climb up and rescue you."

"No!" screamed Eric. "I don't need help.
Just leave me alone - I can do it myself!"
"Fine!" snapped Billy. "Have it your way!"
As he turned his back and stormed away.

At the end of the day young Eric raced
To meet his Grandpa at the gates.
But as he charged at a crazy pace,
He forgot all about his trailing lace...
THUD!!!

Grandpa scraped him off the ground,
Gave him a hug and dusted him down.
Then battered, bruised, dazed and confused,
Eric reviewed the day's bad news:

"Gramps, I've had the worst day ever.
  I wrecked my raft thinking I was clever.
I wouldn't let Miss help with lunch - instead
  I ended up wearing my food on my head!
I got stuck up a tree, then fell to the floor,
  And me and Billy aren't friends any more!
Now I've tripped on my laces and grazed my knees -
  I've had enough, Gramps. Help me please!"

"My dear boy, I have to say
It sounds like pride has wrecked your day!
Always be ready to ask for help -
From teachers, friends, from God himself.
Pride will always make us stumble,
But God gives grace to the truly humble."*

*James 4 v 6

"Then I want grace!" the little lad yelped.
"I need God's help - I can't do it myself!"
Grandpa knelt at Eric's feet.
He laced his sneakers nice and neat.

"So now you've let me tie your laces,
Let's pray to God, 'cos he's where grace is."
"OK", said Eric, "But how do we pray?
How does it work? What should I say?"

"Well," said Gramps, "prayer is how
We talk to God right here and now.
God's a Father who loves and hears us,
If we trust in his Son, Jesus.
You don't need words that are big and smart.
Just be yourself and speaK your heart."

So side by side they started walking.
Eric sighed, then started talking...

"Dear God, here we are,
On the way to Grandpa's car.
I'm sorry for all the times today
I tried to do things my own way.
Forgive me for being so proud and silly.
Please help me sort things out with Billy."

Then just as Eric said, "Amen", Billy bounced around the bend.

Eric froze - his hair stood on end. "I-I'm sorry, Billy. Please be my friend."

"Of course!" said Billy, beaming bright.
"We're bestest buddies - friends for life!"

The boys shook hands and headed home,
Friendship fixed, problem gone.

Eric was buzzin', bamboozled, amazed!
"God just heard the prayer I prayed!"

Smiling, Grandpa ruffled his hair -
"I love it when Father answers prayer!"

A GAME TO PLAY

For a whole day, replace the word
"please" with "cheese".

At the end of the day, take a moment
to reflect on all the "cheese" moments;
note how many times you've needed to
ask for help; then thank God for all the
people who have given it. To finish, say
a special thank you to God for all the
help that he gives in saving, guiding
and providing for us.

A VERSE TO SAY

"When I was in trouble, I called to the Lord.
And he answered me."
(Psalm 120 v 1, International Children's Bible)

A PRAYER TO PRAY*

Loving Father, may your name be blessed,
Do things your way 'cos your way is best.
Provide us with all that we need for today.
Forgive all the wrong things we do, think and say.
Help us forgive as we've been forgiven.
Protect us from evil and lead us to heaven.
Amen.

*Based on Jesus' prayer in
Matthew 6 v 9-13